NEW YORK'S 50 HOTTEST

———

Night

spots

SECOND EDITION

Andrew Essex

CITY & COMPANY
New York

The previous edition was published as *New York's 50
Best Nightspots*.

City & Company
22 West 23rd Street
New York, NY 10010

Creative Coordinator: Kristin Frederickson
Design by Nancy Steiny Design and Jillian Blume Griggs
Electronic Production: Jillian Blume Griggs

Library of Congress Cataloging-in-Publication Data is
available upon request.

Second Edition

ISBN 1-885492-39-1

Printed in the United States of America

Publisher's Note
Neither City & Company nor the author has any
interest, financial or personal, in the locations listed in
this book. No fees were paid or services rendered in
exchange for inclusion in these pages. Please also note
that while every effort was made to ensure that infor-
mation regarding phone numbers, hours and admission fees was accurate at the time of publication, it is
always best to call ahead.

Acknowledgments

Special thanks to the following people whose kindness and wisdom have helped me immensely: Margaret Castaldo, Robert Cavagna, Kevin Conley, Bruce Diones, Hal Espen, Kristin Frederickson, Jillian Blume Griggs, Jeffery Gustavson, Martha Kaplan, James Keller, Bo Niles, Mary Norris, Emily Nunn, Betsey Osborne, Nick Parker, Craig Seligman, Susan Thomsen. And, of course, Roberta Rosenberg. Thanks also to Helene Silver and the crew at City & Company.

Contents

Introduction

In New York, great times are legion, but sometimes, a little help is needed to find them. This book is offered as such an expedient. After all, I do this for a living. I've endured enough punctured eardrums and bad food to weigh in with a reasonable degree of authority.

Several well-known venues have been disqualified for abusive doormen, watered-down drinks, and terrible sightlines. Others seemed in perilous financial straits. Some were too new and untested. But for the most part contestants from every nocturnal genre have been included, from swank cocktail lounges to greasy spoons, from drag bars to glittering dance clubs. Census takers may note that the uptown reaches, particularly the Upper West Side, have been slightly under-represented. I bear no ill will toward the Upper West Side. There are certainly hundreds of great places along Columbus and Amsterdam

Avenues—but nothing that stands out. If I've slandered anyone's neighborhood hang out—please let me know. Still, as Frank Sinatra says, "when you're alone and life is making you lonely, you can always go...Downtown."

Whenever possible, your mantra should be "weekends are for amateurs." Inflated cover charges and uptight crowds can make Friday and Saturday bleak. In an attempt to offer alternatives *The Times* once nominated Thursday as the new "hot" evening to go out. I prefer Sunday, when the weekend warriors are in retreat and the clubs are empty and accommodating. Thus, Sunday is Thursday and Thursday is Friday. Saturday, by contrast is Sunday. Got it?

Good Luck.

A.E.

ART BAR

Address: 52 Eighth Ave. bet. Jane and Horatio Sts.
Phone: 727-0244
Hours: Daily, 4 P.M. to 4 A.M.
Admission: Free

When it first opened, the Art Bar had little to recommend it save for a "foosball" table and a surreal "Rock and Roll Last Supper" mural (Jim Morrison as Christ; Madonna, Andy Warhol, and Marilyn Monroe as the Apostles, etc). These days the mural remains, but everything else has changed.

The Art Bar still looks like a generic down-town pub (except for that painting), but a peek beyond the mysterious black curtain in the back reveals a cozy L-shaped exposed-brick room, sparsely appointed with flowing drapes, potted palms, slouchy couches, and comfortable slipcovered chairs. Candles and

a line of small chandeliers light the room, along with a roaring (gas) fireplace, which gives off enough heat to toast numb toes on a winter's night. Hipsters hunker around tiny octagonal tables or cuddle on the couches. Reading, talking, and taking off your shoes are encouraged: it's the sort of place you want to keep a secret.

The Art Bar has a clever, inexpensive menu (nothing over $8) with hefty portions, and the drinks are equally generous.

Nearby: Nell's (neo-Victorian dance club) at 246 W. 14th St. bet. Seventh & Eighth Aves., 675-1567; Florent (funky and French for 4 A.M. crowd) at 69 Gansevoort St. bet. Greenwich & Washington Sts., 989-5779; Corner Bistro (neighborhood watering hole with burgers and fries) at 331 W. 4th St. at Jane St., 242-9502.

BARNES & NOBLE

Address: 675 Sixth Avenue bet. 21st and 22nd Sts.
Phone: 727-1227
Hours: Daily 9 A.M. to 11:00 P.M.
Admission: Free

It might seem absurd to include a bookstore in a guide to New York nightlife, but the Chelsea branch of Barnes & Noble is the literary equivalent of a night club. Like all their superstores (and new ones seem to be popping up everywhere), Barnes & Noble is open late—until eleven at night, all week long. The extended hours create a bookish singles bar sort of atmosphere and the elevated coffee shoppe affords a birds-eye view of the action.

Latte, cappuccino, biscotti and all manner of trendy snacks are available. You can sit undisturbed for hours and polish off a book without ever paying for it.

Despite its vast size, this branch feels a bit like a cozy living room. There are couches and comfy chairs to slouch on. Business hums along with an unforced disinterest and the unobtrusive staff actually knows a thing or two about books. Many people like to hang around, flipping through the arty nude photography books and making small talk. The latter can get a little turgid, but it's often well worth the effort—Barnes & Noble is probably the only place in New York to meet an intelligent person after 10:45 p.m.

Nearby: Lola (nouveau soul food and occasional live music) at 30 W. 22nd St. bet. Fifth & Sixth Aves., 675-6700; Hot Tomato (eats and drinks until 4 A.M.) at 676 Sixth Ave. at 21st St., 691-3535.

BEACON THEATRE

Address: 2124 Broadway bet. 74th and 75th Sts.
Phone: 496-7070
Admission: Varies.

With its enormous chandelier, gilded proscenium, and ornately detailed masonry, the Beacon is closer in spirit to a landmark Broadway palace than a midlevel concert hall.

The 70-year-old Beaux Arts auditorium caters mostly to that rare breed of artist whose fans are too numerous for gritty clubs and too sparse for grand arenas—recent pilgrims include Emmylou Harris, Lou Reed, and The Mavericks. Concerts are relaxed and well-contained affairs (because of a strict in-house union, the shows always end before 11 P.M.). Don't arrive late unless you deliberately want to miss the opening act; the unfamiliar civility

brings out the best in people. The Beacon has a loge and a balcony section, too, both of which afford excellent views of the action. You may actually prefer sitting upstairs: the ancient chandelier dangles precariously over the orchestra seats.

The Beacon offers reasonably priced snacks like popcorn and hot dogs, and, despite the occasionally muddled sound, it's an excellent place to see a show.

Nearby: Drip (highly-caffeinated singles scene) at 489 Amsterdam Ave. at 83rd St., 875-1032; Prohibition (dining, drinking, and live music nightly) at 503 Columbus Ave. at 84th St., 579-3100; Joe's Fish Shack (down-home beach bar) at 522 Columbus Ave. at 85th St., 873-0341.

BIRDLAND

Address: 315 W. 44th bet. Eighth and Ninth Aves.
Phone: 581-3080
Hours: Friday and Saturday, 5 P.M. to 1 A.M.,
Sunday through Thursday, 5 P.M. to Midnight
Admission: Friday and Saturday,
cover charge (varies with music).

In November, this legendary jazz club named after Charlie Parker moved back downtown (close to its original location on 52nd Street) and it has started to "sing" again.

While the yellow and orange neon club continues to offer its popular menu, the emphasis at this Birdland is on the music and the clamoring musicians are sounding their approval. The space has been carefully designed to create consistently excellent sightlines and acoustics that favor the sounds emanating from the stage rather than the audience. Perch atop one of the high stools at the dimly-lit horseshoe-shaped

bar to the right of the stage or take a seat at one of the candlelit tables on the main floor, where on one of three semi-circular tiers, the remarkably silent waitresses—Birdland has a "quiet policy" during performances—will take your order.

Birdland does, however, remain one of those rare jazz clubs where the kitchen actually competes with the musicians. There's a wonderful low-country/soul menu and spacious seating. Pay particular attention to the bourbon-glazed tuna and the catfish poboys. Shows are $10–30, depending on the musicians and there is a food and drink minimum of $10.

Nearby: Revolution (all-night happy hour) at 611 Ninth Ave. bet. 43rd & 44th Sts., 489-8451; Rudy's (old-man bar gone cool) at 627 Ninth Ave. bet. 44th & 45th Sts., 974-9169.

BLUE NOTE

Address: 131 W. 3rd St.
bet. Sixth Ave. and Thompson St.
Phone: 475-8592
Hours: Daily, doors open at 7 P.M.,
Showtimes 9 P.M., 11:30 P.M.
Admission: Varies with each band (call to check).

The McDonalds of all jazz clubs, the Blue Note now owns franchises in Tokyo and Jakarta, and like Mickey D's, they serve up a little meat and a little cheese. The meat is the endless array of high quality marquee bookings such as the Count Basie Big Band, Lionel Hampton, and even a rare appearance by Dave Brubeck—and the club has an almost metaphysical ability to keep them coming and coming.

There are two performances a night. Whenever possible, you should opt for the late show. That's when the bands are more

relaxed, and the club doesn't have to rush you away from your table. The cheese, unfortunately, refers to the conspicuous allotment of mirrors and the presence of a gift shop on the second floor, which sells, among other things, Blue Note belt buckles for your relatives Out in New Jersey and Beyond. Still, who can fault a club for cashing in on tourist fever? Actually, it's sort of charming.

Ask for a table with access to an aisle—it can get a little cramped here—and you'll have a blast.

Nearby: Cornelia Street Café (cozy jazz bistro) at 29 Cornelia Street bet. W. 4th & Bleecker Sts., 989-9318; Life (disco of the moment) 158 Bleecker Street bet. Thompson & Sullivan Sts., 420-1999.

BOWERY BAR AND GRILL

Address: 40 E. 4th St.
bet. Lafayette St. and Bowery
Phone: 475-2220
Hours: Daily, 11 A.M. to 4 A.M.
Admission: Free

Like the Merc Bar (p.72), the Bowery Bar has seen the moment of its greatness flicker—and the world is a better place: a little humility goes a long way in New York. Still, for the first half of 1994, this former gas station turned swank bistro was strictly for the holier-than-thou set. If you did manage to get in, there was a very good chance of seeing a supermodel, and this kind of excitement brought out the worst in people.

These days the foreboding concrete exterior and the striking orange Christmas lights (where the gas pumps used to be) make a visit to the Bowery Bar an exciting event, and the

surplus glamour compels the maître d' to inquire, "do you have a reservation?" Fortunately, this is just a ruse, a vestige from the glory days; in fact, you're quickly seated and pleasantly served.

Admire the burnt-orange mood lighting, the swollen paper light fixtures, the lush plant life, and the old rusted gears mounted on the walls like objets d'art. The food is pretty good, too.

Nearby: KGB (beloved pseudo-communist drinking hole) at 85 E. 4th St., 505-3360; Global 33 (restaurant/bar with DJ) at 93 Second Ave. bet. 5th & 6th Sts., 477-8427; Lucky Cheng's (Chinese food served by drag queens) at 24 First Ave. bet. 1st & 2nd Sts., 473-0516.

BOWLMOR

**Address: 110 University Pl.,
bet. 12th and 13th Sts.
Phone: 255-8188
Hours: Sunday through Thursday, 10 A.M. to 1 A.M.;
Friday and Saturday, 10 A.M. to 4 A.M.
Prices: $3.25 per game; $1 for shoes.**

Visitors to Bowlmor are guaranteed forty-four lanes and a glimpse of the Simpler Days genially evoked by TV reruns like *Happy Days* and *Laverne and Shirley*. You can enter only via an ancient, slow-moving elevator that inches to the fourth floor. When the doors open, you will be blasted by the heartwarming thunder of bowling balls crushing pins, dazzled by the sight of homey wood paneling, scuffed linoleum floors, and floating clouds of cigarette smoke.

C

Slip on a pair of bowling shoes old enough to belong in the Smithsonian and observe that

there are real waitresses carrying beer and greasy snacks to every table. Note that the diverse crowd appears to be having a great time (even though the overhead scoreboards are out-of-order.)

Bowlmor has a vast collection of bowling balls, including lightweights for amateurs and weaklings. Inveterate bowl-a-phobes can always take shelter in the bar/cafeteria area—the special of the house is grilled cheese—or just mess around with the antiquated video games.

Nearby: Japonica (one of the best Japanese restaurants in NYC) at 100 University Pl. bet. 12th & 13th Sts., 243-7752; Coffee Shop (old diner with vampy crowd) at 29 Union Sq. W. at 16th St., 243-7969.

BROWNIES

Address: 169 Ave. A, bet. 10th and 11th Sts.
Phone: 420-8392
Hours: Daily 5 P.M. to 2 A.M.
Admission: Varies with each band
(call to check).

Despite recent attempts at gentrification, the East Village—particularly everything east of First Avenue—is for some as exotic and intimidating as the Congo. This is a mistake, as anyone who's visited Brownies will tell you. The musical epicenter of Alphabet City for more than five years, Brownies has gradually evolved into a surprisingly pleasant, clean—and astoundingly professional—operation.

A Generation X mating ground, the club is frequented by brooding college students and a small contingent of the pierced-nostril set.

In addition to its groovy violet lava-lamp ambiance, amenities such as ventilation, a real stage, and a P.A. system loud enough to compete with a beer-soaked, bare-chested drummer have been successfully addressed.

On any given night, expect five or six different combos, with the headliner in the clean-up slot. Near the stage you'll find a handful of tables, which give way to a single bar with a whimsical pressed-tin motif. The bar is generously stocked with upscale beer and other high-quality concoctions.

Nearby: Stingy Lulu's (24-hour luncheonette) at 129 St. Mark's Pl. bet. A & First Aves., 674-3545; Vazac's (landmark dive bar) at 108 Ave. B & 7th St., 473-8840.

CAFÉ CARLYLE BEMELMANS BAR

IN THE CARLYLE HOTEL

Address: 36 E. 76th St. bet. Madison and Park Aves.
Phone: 744-1600
Hours: Café Carlyle—Tuesday through Saturday,
6:30 P.M. to 1 A.M.; Bemelmans Bar—
Monday through Saturday, 11 A.M. to 2 A.M.
Admission: Café Carlyle—$45 per person, no
minimum **Showtimes:** 8:45 P.M. and 10:45 P.M.;
Bemelmans Bar—After 9:30 P.M.,
$10 cover per person, no minimum.

In a classic sequence from *Hannah and Her Sisters*, Woody Allen takes a coked-up Dianne Weist to the Carlyle to see Bobby Short after an abortive visit to CBGB's (see p. 30). Art imitates life: Woody Allen is a fixture at Bobby Short's opening night. And for good reason. A visit to the Café Carlyle during one of Mr. Short's performances is one of the obligatory Manhattan experiences. At the Carlyle you can enjoy officious service from waiters in white jackets and black neckties and have the chance to order things like oysters Rockefeller

with a straight face, all the while admiring the pastel walls bedecked with a fantastic neo-Degas theme. Gentlemen are required to wear jackets. (On one occasion, I observed a waiter reproach a man for taking off his jacket. It happened to be unusually warm that evening, but rules are rules.)

If you're meeting someone before the show, get together across the hall in the delightful Bemelmans Bar. Here you'll find a time-capsule vision of New York that seems right out of F. Scott Fitzgerald. Bemelmans is intimate, civilized, and distinguished. You can sit at the bar or on a puckered red leather banquette and admire the whimsical illustrated wallpaper by Ludwig Bemelmans, the great Austrian writer and painter. Smack in the middle of the room there's a baby grand piano and a suave pianist for your listening pleasure.

CAROLINES

Address: 1626 Broadway bet. 49th and 50th St.
Phone: 757-4100
Hours: Monday through Friday, 5 P.M. to 7 P.M.
(Happy Hour); Saturday and Sunday, opens 6 P.M.
Showtimes: Sunday through Thursday, 8 P.M.,
10:30 P.M.; Friday, 8 P.M., 11 P.M.; Saturday 8 P.M.,
10:30 P.M.; Closing time, 1/2 hour after last show
Admission: $10.00 to $20.00 depending on show,
plus a 2 drink minimum. Reservations required.

Steve Martin once said "Comedy is not pretty" and he wasn't fooling around. For the most part, live comedy is a depressing affair—a collection of mediocre talents competing for the spotlight while the audience sits and fidgets with their drinks.

Fortunately, Caroline's has established itself as New York's preeminent comedy joint, a classy well-run organization that keeps the stage packed with well-known and up-and-coming acts. You walk down a steep cast-iron staircase

and enter a dark blue on blue neon bar area that looks like a dance club, an illusion perpetuated by dance videos playing on the monitors. The walls are festooned with mock-Avedon black-and-white portraits of former guests headliners: Richard Belzer, Jerry Seinfeld, and Jackie Mason.

Seating begins about a half-hour before the show (there are two sets on weekends) and you find yourself inside a small auditorium decorated with a multicolored argyle motif and a long, arcing collection of banquettes and rainbow drapery. There's a light menu, with pizza and a selection of dippable items.

Nearby: Virgin Records (megastore in Times Square) at 1540 Broadway at 45th St., 921-1020.

CBGB/CB'S GALLERY

Address: 315 Bowery,
bet. Bleecker and Great Jones Sts.
Phone: 982-4052
Hours: CBGB—Sunday and Monday, 7 P.M. to
2 A.M.; Tuesday through Thursday, 7 P.M. to
2 A.M.; Friday and Saturday, 8 P.M. to 4 A.M.;
CB's Gallery—Daily, 7 P.M. to 3 A.M.
Admission: CBGB—Tuesday and Wednesday, $5;
Thursday, $7; Friday and Saturday, $9,
depending on band;
CB's Gallery—$5-$7 for music,
depending on player.

If only for its historical significance, everyone should make at least one pilgrimage to CBGB's. CB's really is something of a museum—or at least the closest New York has to offer to the real Rock and Roll Hall of Fame in Cleveland. One must Never Forget that this celebrated cavern is the petri dish of Punk and that these slime encrusted walls still contain trace droppings of a huge musical anti-movement that has been one of the defining facets of American culture.

These days, like most museums, CB's has grown a bit stuffy and moribund, but the club soldiers on, uninterested in renovation, its wall growing thicker every year with new graffiti. Of course, none of this should discourage anyone in search of some serious head-pounding.

In the past few years, to make up for the stalactites and the stagnation, CBGB's has opened an impressive, remarkably clean annex called CB's gallery, which serves as a showcase for art and the more esoteric ramblings of smaller, avant-garde ensembles and the odd spoken-word engagement.

Nearby: Bleecker Street Bar (lively pub) at 56 Bleecker St. bet. Lafayette & Crosby Sts., 334-0244.

CHELSEA BILLIARDS

Address: 54 W. 21st St. bet. Fifth and Sixth Aves.
Phone: 989-0096
Hours: Open 24 hours.
Admission: Sunday through Thursday, after
5 P.M., $5 an hour (1 player), $10 an hour
(2+ players), $2 for each additional player;
Friday and Saturday, $6 an hour (1 player),
$14 an hour (2+ players).

Salmon isn't the color I'd paint my pool room (after all, it clashes horribly with baize), but the action at Chelsea Billiards is usually dazzling enough to distract you from the horrendous decor.

How can anyone complain about a place that remains open twenty-four hours, where you can play Eight Ball at four-thirty in the morning and Nine Ball at eight A.M.? The frills here are few and far between: no alcohol, no juke box (management picks the tunes), just a few cheesy vending machines for fruit juice,

snacks, and cigarettes, and a set of pool cue safe deposit boxes.

There are about three dozen tables, all dimly lit by dangling fluorescent fixtures, and the acne-pink walls are dotted with pictures from the Pool Shark Hall of Fame. The crowd is concerned but not fanatical; serious players stand side by side with giggling hacks.

If you're interested in learning how to hustle, there's a pool school on Tuesday afternoons, but you're better off just watching the pros. Snooker goes down in the back.

Nearby: Zip City Brewing Co. (freshly brewed beer) at 3 W. 18th St. bet. Fifth & Sixth Aves., 366-6333.

CHESTNUT ROOM

Address: Central Park West, bet. 67th and 68th Sts.
Phone: 873-3200
Hours: Vary, see Showtimes
Showtimes: Tuesday, Wednesday, Thursday and
Sunday, 8 P.M. and 9:30 P.M.; Friday and
Saturday, 8:30 P.M. and 10 P.M.
Admission: $5 cover every night; No minimum.

The Chestnut Room looks something like Liberace's hunting lodge: glass walls, glitter, electrified trees, wood beams, kitschy mementos, trophies, and a dozen chandeliers. But for the past few years, it's been home to some of the best jazz acts around.

Begin your evening with a long, appetite-building sunset walk in the park. Then step inside. Snag a table near the action: jaw-dropping regulars include the great singer Little Jimmy Scott, piano giant Tommy Flanagan, and saxophonist

Illinois Jacquet. The band lays it down on a small stage no bigger than one at a provincial Elks Club. Virtually every seat affords a delicious up-close and personal view of the performers and the Park—although the preponderance of garish jewelry and electric blue hair is just as stunning as any saxophone solo. The food is all fairly good (though meat and potato creations are recommended over fancier, more challenging dishes).

After the show, you can walk around the labyrinthine corridors of the rest of the club, stop by the gift shop for a miniature steel Empire State Building—or crash a wedding or two. Make a night of it. But take care not to get lost—the Tavern on the Green is huge, and, like the Port Authority, tour buses are constantly departing.

CHICAGO BLUES

Address: 73 Eighth Ave. bet. 13th and 14th Sts.
Phone: 924-9755
Hours: Daily, 5 P.M. through 2 A.M.
Showtimes: Around 9:30 P.M.; 11:30 P.M.; 12:30 A.M.
Admission: Sunday through Tuesday, no cover;
Wednesday, $7; Thursday, $7;
Friday and Saturday, $15.

Plastered with old records, street signs, vintage South Side memorabilia, and an oversized poster of John Belushi, Chicago Blues has been conceived as an authentic slice of Windy City night life for this blues-starved city.

Wednesday through Saturday the club imports heavy-duty acts straight "outta" Illinois—Big Time Sarah and the BTS Express, Luther "Guitar" Johnson, Smoky Smothers, for starters—to recreate the musical equivalent of pain and suffering for your listening pleasure.

For consistency the club has been painted a "lonesome ocean" blue, and every funky accoutrement from rotating fans to an old deco jukebox is part of the scene. Unlike most half-baked blues joints, Chicago Blues is decidedly top-shelf.

Each show features three long sets, which begin promptly at 9:30; you clearly get your money's worth at Chicago Blues. Expect friendly service, safety, and excellent sound. On Sundays, there's a blues jam for neighborhood oddities. Mondays and Tuesdays are given over to local acts.

Nearby: Joyce Theatre (avant-dance headquarters) at 175 Eighth Ave. at 19th St., 242-0800; Rebar (basic dj, dancing, and drinking) at 127 Eighth Ave. at 16th St., 627-1680; Rio Mar (cheap Spanish fare) at 7 Ninth Ave. at Little W. 12th St., 242-1623.

CONEY ISLAND HIGH

Address: 15 St. Marks Pl.
Phone: 674-7959
Hours: Daily, 5 P.M. to 4 A.M.
Admission: Varies with band (call to check).

Situated smack in the middle of darkest St. Marks Place—New York's definitive postapocalyptic thoroughfare—this no-frills temple of tortured guitars and ear-sizzling cymbals has an amusing, let's-wing-it charm and a functional purposefulness that would make I. M. Pei smile.

On your way in, you'll pass through a blood-red entrance way, pay a nominal fee, and step into a sea of black that's set off by a half dozen red Tiki lamps and a baby blue snack bar, where you can purchase nutritious club fare like Dipsy Doodles and Snickers. Coney Island High's greatest accomplishment (besides nam-

ing itself after the legendary amusement park) is the frightening collage of black-lacquered detritus that hangs over the bar—it looks like something from the set of Aliens.

Like most rock clubs these days, Coney Island hosts two or three theme nights. Mondays feature a d.j.-driven fantasia of twitchy drum 'n bass dance music from England. Saturdays are either Green Door NYC, Corruption, or Havana. Call to check.

Nearby: @ Café (coffee and computers) at 12 St. Mark's Place, 979-5439; Pommes Frites (European-style french fries until 11 P.M., 1 A.M. on weekends) at 123 Second Ave., 674-1234.

THE COOLER

Address: 416 W. 14th St. bet. Ninth and Tenth Aves.
Phone: 229-0785
Hours: Daily, 8 P.M. to 4 A.M.
Showtimes: Monday through Thursday, 9 P.M.;
Friday and Saturday, 10 P.M.; Sunday,
call regarding special events.
Admission: Monday, no charge;
Tuesday through Sunday, $10 maximum.

The city certainly has no shortage of bars doubling as meat markets, but the idea of using a real meat cooler, complete with rusty old hooks and a huge butcher's scale, was a twisted stroke of genius. The Cooler fancies itself something of a hipsters' paradise: you enter through an unmarked neon portal, descend a staircase, and find yourself in a slick, incandescent, purple and stainless-steel catacomb lined with banquets and black-and-white photographs. The Cooler has a small single stage, half a dozen candle-lit tables, and two bars. A few back rooms fill nightly with black-clad artist types deep in conversation.

The atmosphere here is laid-back and self-congratulatory: meaningful glances are frequently exchanged. The musical fare is Bohemian deluxe. Wednesday nights, alternately called "Chiaroscuro" and "Night of the Living Dub," are given over to ambient, experimental d.j. projects, such as "Liquid Sky"—a style that percolates at a conversation-friendly volume.

Monday nights are free, with rotating "curators" who tend to fancy apocalyptic sonic collages. Weekends have been known to feature alternative-rock, world-music, punk-jazz—and all of the above. The Cooler also has a semi-regular series of silent films with live accompaniment.

Nearby: Hogs and Heifers (raucous pseudo-biker bar) at 859 Washington St., 929-0655.

CONTINENTAL CLUB

AT IRVING PLAZA

Address: 17 Irving Place bet. 15th and 16th Sts.
Phone: 696-9737
Hours: Sunday, 7 P.M. to 12 A.M.
Showtime: 8 P.M.
Admission: $12, general; $4, seniors; $8, Swing
Dance Society members. Band varies (call to check).

Every Sunday evening Irving Plaza, a renovated burlesque theater that's usually home to an unpredictable mix of snarling, hardcore bands and world-music aficionados, hands the reins over to the Swing Dance Society, an organization rabidly devoted to the preservation of "swing dancing to live Big Band music."

The SDS proudly hangs their banner over the club's marquee, puts an honest-to-God big band on the stage and, as the sounds of Count Basie, Jimmy Lunceford, and other

Savoy Ballroom greats fill the air, the dancing begins. The big favorite happens to be the Lindy, but don't be intimidated; the crowd is as diverse in demographics as it is in skill. Don't expect to see Tommy Tune. If you don't know how to Lindy, fake it (though lessons are available). Most of the crowd seems blissfully amateurish, with a few ringers sprinkled about, just to keep everyone honest.

If you don't dance, you can sit upstairs in the balcony and check out the action or just hang in the pleasant deco-ish back room, where dancers of all ages rest their aching dogs.

Nearby: Café Beulah (excellent low-country food) at 39 E. 19th St. bet. Broadway & Park Ave., 777-9700.

DENIM & DIAMONDS

Address: 511 Lexington Ave. bet. 47th and 48th Sts.
Phone: 371-1600
Hours: Monday through Friday, 7 P.M. to 4 A.M.;
Saturday and Sunday, 7 P.M. to 4 A.M.
Admission: Thursday, $5 cover after 8 P.M.;
Friday and Saturday, $8 cover after 8 P.M.
Sunday through Wednesday, no cover charge.

John Travolta is back and so is this over-the-top midtown saloon for urban cowboys and cowgirls. There's no mechanical bull, unfortunately, but all the other ersatz dude ranch trappings are intact. Vide: rawhide and palomino banquettes, stage coach wheels, lassos, spurs, cacti, comely waitresses, and huge bouncers in ten-gallon hats.

The crowd seems to be primarily young urban professionals with a yearning for the prairies. Forget about stools; steers just saddle up to the bar for a beer and brand their loved ones,

while the crowd bobs to a non-stop set of Merle Haggard and Johnny Cash tunes.

Everyone has that sort of I-can't-believe-I'm-really-digging-this sort of grin, and the crowd is friendly and relaxed. Downstairs there are several small rooms, a few pool tables, and an octagonal dance floor (sort of like a rodeo ring) for line dancing, but check your spurs at the door. There's also a remarkably well-stocked gift shop, should you be inclined to get yo'sef a hat.

Nearby: Tatou (midtown supper club) at 151 E. 50th St. bet. Lexington & Third Aves., 753-1144.

DUPLEX

Address: 61 Christopher St.
bet. Sixth and Seventh Aves.
Phone: 255-5438
Hours: Daily, 4 P.M. to 4 A.M.
Admission: Varies (call to check). Cash only.

I t's always Christmas at Duplex, Armageddon, too. Duplex is the unofficial headquarters for the Wigstock crowd and the irrepressible Lady Bunny, and there's enough oscillating strobe light and disco ball dazzle going on here to wake the dead.

Camp is the operative word here, and camp is what you get: the bartender thrusts a microphone in your face, encouraging sing-a-longs with Liza. A spirit of blythe adventure characterizes all the activities. The bartender fast-forwards the tape player (via remote control) because the music is boring somebody. Free drinks are served from a set of test tubes.

Everyone seems to know each other. This is one of the friendliest places in New York. Upstairs at Duplex there's a cabaret space that features programmed entertainment not necessarily appropriate for Grandma. On any given night you can count on seeing someone with a shaved chest engage in some form of "anything goes" abandon. But the adventures are always ambi-sexual and strictly on the level of innuendo.

If you're bored by the aforementioned, you can always chat up the club's psychic coat check.

Nearby: Small's (aptly named jazz bar) at 183 W. 10th St. at Seventh Ave., 929-7565; Boxer's (cozy pub) at 186 W. 4th St. bet. Sixth & Seventh Aves., 633-2275.

FEZ

Address: 380 Lafayette St.
bet. E. 4th and Great Jones Sts.
Phone: 533-7000
Hours: Bar, Sunday through Thursday, 6 P.M. to
2 A.M.; Friday and Saturday, 6 P.M. to 4 A.M.
Admission: Varies with musical event.

Discreetly tucked away inside the diner-cum-restaurant called Time Café, Fez is a warm, split-level bar and performance space with an identity crisis. A walk through the restaurant's brightly lit dining area leads you into what appears to be an opium parlor in Northern Morocco.

Comfort is the key at Fez, and everyone seems to be in various degrees of slouch. There are thick rugs, lots of squishy, rickety sofas, beaded curtains, moody indirect lighting, and murmuring conversation. Fez is the sort of place where you'd expect to spot William

Burroughs, Allen Ginsberg, and Paul Bowles sitting around in wrinkled white linen suits scribbling in their journals and drinking quinine.

The downstairs room, where you'll find live music and other conceptual performances, is pleasant if unremarkable: a few gold lamé trappings, a small stage, a dozen cozy booths and tables, and an unobtrusive bar in the back.

If for some reason you don't like the music—the emphasis here is on tiny eclectic combos—go back upstairs to the bar area, have an absinthe, and look thoughtful.

Nearby: Temple Bar (dinosaur-embossed watering hole) at 332 Lafayette St., 925-4242; Indochine (airy Vietnamese eatery) at 430 Lafayette St., 505-5111.

FIFTY-SEVEN FIFTY-SEVEN

IN THE FOUR SEASONS HOTEL

Address: 57 E. 57th St. bet. Park and Madison Aves.
Phone: 758-5757
Hours: Piano Bar—Monday through Thursday,
7 P.M. to 2 A.M.; Friday and Saturday, 6 P.M. to
9 P.M., followed by a Jazz Trio from 9 P.M. to
1 A.M.; Admission: $20 cover.
Dinner Hours—Daily, 6 P.M. to 10:30 P.M.;
Bar Hours—Daily to 1 A.M.

Here's the skinny: your significant other's parents are coming in from Out There. They're conservative (but not embalmed), and they expect a New York–style good time. You don't have a Rainbow Room–sized budget but you want to go somewhere special before dinner or after curtain call at Les Mis.

57

Your prayers have been answered! Make haste to Fifty-Seven Fifty-Seven, the swank and sybaritic piano bar and café in the polymorphously deluxe

Four Seasons Hotel. Like one of those make-believe night clubs that used to appear in old films about New York, there's a regal twenty-five foot ceiling, an elegant cherry wood bar stocked with rare, twenty-year-old Scotch, a talented pianist tossing off jazz standards, and an efficient wait staff ready to cater to your every whim.

Upon seating, your table is dressed with a bowl of delicious crackers and savory olives, and you are encouraged to try the specialty of the house: the martini and every imaginative permutation thereof, from the original gin-and-vermouth number to postmodern fruit-and-liqueur variations—all served in a goblet deep enough to make blissfully tolerable even the most insufferable of potential in-laws.

Nearby: Trattoria dell'Arte (Italian dining and celeb sightings) at 900 Seventh Ave. bet. 56th & 57th Sts., 245-9800.

GRAMERCY TAVERN

Address: 42 E. 20th St.
bet. Park Ave. S. and Broadway
Phone: 477-0777
Hours: Sunday through Thursday, Noon to
11 P.M.; Friday and Saturday, Noon to Midnight.

Despite the fact that *The Times* only gave it two stars and the benefit of the doubt, New York's newest four-star restaurant-manqué remains a hotbed of upscale posing and culinary feats of derring-do.

🍴

If you're interested in infiltrating a restaurant that reserves its tables two months in advance (but you lack the appropriate cash-flow), grab a slatted leather stool or a table by the lacquered black bar. Here you can order a beer and try one of several inexpensive "Tavern Tastes,"—such as quail with polenta or lamb sandwiches with aioli—and still manage to observe the lurid feeding rituals of the beautiful

people (and the Armani-clad wait staff), without ever setting foot in the exorbitantly priced main dining area.

If the human comedy should bore you, there's always the multi-colored Warholian fruit painting that runs along the perimeter of the ceiling and the faux-wood beams that subtly remind you that people are actually spending large sums of money to eat in a tavern.

Nearby: No Idea (archetypal neighborhood bar) at 30 E. 20th St. bet. Broadway & Park Ave., 777-0100; Patria (delicious Nuevo Latino cuisine) at 250 Park Ave. S. at 20th St., 777-6211; Metronome (nightclub with dance music) at 915 Broadway at 21st St., 505-7400.

THE GREATEST BAR ON EARTH

1 World Trade Center at
Windows on the World Restaurant
Phone: 524-7000
Hours: Thursday to Saturday live entertainment
from 9 P.M., last set at 11:45 P.M.; piano player
from 5 P.M. to 9 P.M.
Admission: $5 music charge at the bar, $10 at
tables. Note: no jeans, sneakers, or t-shirts
before 9 P.M.

Here is the answer to the eternal question: Where can I bring my cousins from Texas? Though the Greatest Bar certainly errs on the side of hyperbole, it's hard to argue with any nightclub that features a panoramic view from the hundred-and-sixth floor of one of the tallest buildings on the planet along with a glass of twenty-year-old port. So call it the tallest bar on earth instead and bring all the Texans you can find (they'll feel right at home—most of the crowd is from out of town anyway). The more-is-better ethos extends to the menu, which includes snacks, finger foods,

sushi, and sundry hors d'oeuvres; the choices are few in number but gargantuan in size.

Live music—jazz trios, funk bands, and, every once in a while, the fine Dixieland swing of the Flying Neutrinos—can be heard Thursdays through Saturdays. And though the decor is an ill-conceived salmon-and-mauve horror, on a clear day you can see forever. Or New Jersey, at least.

Nearby: Bubble Lounge (champagne bar) at 228 W. Broadway bet. Franklin & White Sts., 431-3433; Odeon (classic cool restaurant, good for celeb spottings) at 145 W. Broadway at Thomas St., 233-0507.

IBIS

Address: 327 W. 44th St. bet. Eighth and Ninth Aves.
Phone: 262-1111
Hours: Tuesday through Sunday, 6:30 P.M. to 4 A.M.
Showtime: 9:30 P.M.
Admission: $45 per person (includes dinner);
$10 cover, $20 minimum per person.

Decorated like King Tut's midtown bachelor pad, Cleopatra's may be the city's only full-service belly dancing and whirling dervish establishment. While you feast on excellent Middle Eastern comestibles, a small band takes the stage. As a raga begins to bubble, three scantily-clad young ladies appear on the dance floor. Belly dancing, as most know, involves a great deal of undulating and profound hip action.

The whirling dervish, whose appearance is timed shortly after the arrival of your entrée, proceeds to whirl, and whirl—and whirl. It is

like nothing you've ever seen before. As he picks up speed, the dervish begins to gracefully toss off garments that resemble cloth hoola-hoops while he maintains perfect equilibrium. Someone, you notice, sings in the background.

The dervish spins faster and faster. Your mouth opens in amazement and a mild tinge of nausea settles in your stomach. Then, as the music reaches a crescendo, the dervish suddenly stops, exquisitely balanced, and you're on your feet cheering. After a brief break, the belly dancers return, and the tourist contingent takes it upon themselves to throw dollar bills. Participation is not compulsory.

Nearby: Joe Allen (chorus line hangout) at 326 W. 46th St. bet. Eighth & Ninth Aves., 581-6464.

IRIDIUM

Address: 44 W. 63rd St.
bet. Columbus Ave. and Broadway
Phone: 582-2121
Hours: Daily, 8:30 P.M. to Midnight or 1 A.M.
(late night menu).
Showtimes: 8:30, 10:30,
and Midnight on Saturday.
Admission: Varies for jazz club (call to check).

Proof positive that hallucinogenic drugs do irreparable damage, Iridium has erupted on the drab streetscape opposite Lincoln Center as a sort of architectural homage to the Spirit of Alternative Realities.

The motif here is neo-Dali: there isn't a single straight edge in the place. If you're prone to sea-sickness, this is probably not the right place to visit. The tables, couches, columns, and fixtures are the sort of Surrealist melted-cheese configurations that one tends to observe after lengthy international flights. Inexplicably, the

musical fare at Iridium is not psychedelic-era Jefferson Airplane but, rather, it is authentic neo-conservative jazz with an emphasis on emerging artists a step or two from the big time.

The music is performed expertly downstairs in Iridium's nightclub (upstairs is a restaurant/bar area), which has plenty of room but retains an intimate quality. The proximity to Lincoln Center makes for a particularly diverse crowd. Most nights you'll find an opera lover or two mixed in with the jazz-heads.

There are generally two shows a night, and, despite the distraction of the decor, the quality and raucous spirit of the music is well worth it.

Nearby: Cafe des Artistes (romantic classic) at 1 W. 67th St. bet. Columbus & CPW, 877-3500.

KNICKERBOCKER

Address: 33 University Pl., bet. 9th and 10th Sts.
Phone: 228-8490
Hours: Tuesday through Thursday, 11:45 A.M. to
1 A.M.; Friday and Saturday, 11:45 A.M. to 2 A.M.,
Sunday, 11:45 A.M. to Midnight
Showtime: 9:30 or 9:45 P.M.
Admission: Varies (call to check).

This convivial bistro is probably not for hard-core jazz purists—the conversational noise level can get a bit overpowering—but it's certainly one of the best places to go for good food and excellent music (generally of the conservative piano, bass, and drums variety.)

You don't have to applaud after every number, nor worry that you'll be thrown out for dropping your fork during the bass solo. There's no pressure at Knickerbocker, and the bustling good cheer has a lot to do with the burnished

brass rails and the colorful vintage prints that adorn the wheat and mahogany walls. There's also a shoehorn-shaped bar with a few stools that wrap around the small performance area in the near end of the dining room.

As the evening progresses, the chatting and the chime of cutlery is occasionally stifled by the crash of a cymbal or a particularly fine piano fill, and there's a moment of respectful silence. Then everyone returns happily to their food and drink and the enthusiastic conversation begins anew.

Nearby: Dean & DeLuca espresso bar (open late) at 75 University Pl. at 11th St., 473-1908; Bayomo (Cuban-Chinese and great margaritas) at 704 Broadway bet. 4th St. & Washington Pl., 475-5151; Polyester's (retro bar with Brady Bunch photos) at 186 W. 4th St., 924-5707.

THE KNITTING FACTORY

Address: 74 Leonard St.
bet. Broadway and Church St.
Phone: 219-3055
Hours: Vary (call to check).
Showtimes: 8 P.M., 9 P.M., 11 P.M.
Admission: $8 to $20 depending on show.

Once upon a time the Knitting Factory was synonymous with squealing avant-noise combos and cramped, smoky discomfort. But now, thanks to the club's new three-story digs in Tribeca, the Knitting Factory has become a glimmering musical palace.

Whereas the old Knitting Factory served up warm beer and stale air, the club now offers eighteen lines of exotic micro-brewed beer. There's a well-ventilated bar and lounge area in which to hide when the music becomes a bit too adventurous and also a small bar up front with no cover charge and a generous Happy Hour.

If you're there specifically for the music, you have three options: the spacious main room, for seating close to the stage; the balcony area, with theater-style reclining seats that wrap around the baluster, affording an excellent view of the action; and the AlterKnit Theatre, a small, sound-proof second stage devoted to lesser-known experimental projects and spoken-word adventures.

The Knit probably books the most diverse selection of music in the entire city, and on any given night the music can range from transcendent to truly terrible.

Nearby: El Teddy's (upscale Tex-Mex) at 291 W. Broadway bet. Franklin & White Sts., 941-7070; TriBeCa Grill (DeNiro's joint) at 375 Greenwich St. at Franklin St., 941-3900.

LAUTERBACH'S BROOKLYN BEAT

Address: 335 Prospect Ave., Park Slope, Brooklyn
Phone: 718-788-9140
Hours: Daily, 5 P.M. to 3 A.M.
Admission: Saturday night only, $3.

If Archie Bunker ran a nightclub, this would be his place. Situated in the unremarkable outback of Park Slope, in what appears to be (and actually is) a basement apartment, Lauterbach's has long been a musical incubator for New York bands.

The Bunker factor manifests itself in the no-frills, meat-and-potatoes-in-the-rec-room school of hospitality: don't ask for a wine spritzer at Lauterbach's, unless you're a meathead and enjoy being ridiculed.

Go with the flow, and have a beer, a Jack

Daniels, or, if you're on the wagon, coffee from a pot that's been simmering since the Carter administration. (Lauterbach's is not completely immune to the winds of fashion; they'll happily put a shot of Jack Daniels in your coffee.)

The club fancies "theme" evenings, and the best nights feature smallish, talented acoustic combos. Other nights are devoted to Celtic music and alternative rock. It's all very much a family affair, and, provided you can ingratiate yourself with the bartender, you'll find yourself a welcome addition to the family.

Nearby: Cucina (Italian at great prices) at 256 Fifth Ave. bet. Carroll St. & Garfield Pl., 718-230-0711; Park Slope Brewery (neighborhood brew pub) at Sixth Ave. & 5th St., 718-788-1756.

LES POULETS

Address: 16 W. 22nd St.
bet. Fifth and Sixth Aves.
Phone: 229-2000
Hours: Wednesday through Friday, 6 P.M. to 4 A.M.;
Saturday, 9 P.M. to 4 A.M.
Admission: $5 minimum (price varies).

Les Poulets is not (despite its name) a French club, but rather New York's premiere Latin music nightspot. The vibe here might be best described as Club Med noir—the walls are painted in the festive colors of over-ripe papaya and mango (which blends admirably with the obligatory strobe lights and disco balls), and the tables are set apart by cabana-like subdivisions—but there's nothing dilettante about Les Poulets.

Weekends you can almost always find an international star of the caliber of Tito Rodriguez or Tony Vega in the house, and an upscale

Hispanic crowd is here to hear authentic, exquisitely performed salsa.

Because there are no other venues in central Manhattan that offer such high-quality performers for such a huge, under-represented constituency, Les Poulets has a bit of an overcrowding problem, and this occasionally results in a long line outside and a bracing bodily search upon entering. Still, it's usually worth the wait.

Beneath the main performance area there's another dance floor and a restaurant that specializes in the club's namesake: chicken in several tangy grilled styles.

Nearby: Tramps Café (Cajun cuisine), at 45 W. 21st St. bet. Fifth & Sixth Aves., 633-4750.

MANNY'S CAR WASH

Address: 1558 Third Ave.
bet. 87th and 88th Sts.
Phone: 369-2583
Hours: Sunday through Thursday, 5 P.M. to 2 A.M.;
Friday and Saturday, 4 P.M. to 4 A.M.
Showtime: 9:30 P.M.
Admission: Varies with band.

No soap bubbles and scrub brushes here, just a packed crowd of overzealous, well-groomed Upper Eastsiders hungry for the blues.

And the blues is what you get in this beer-soaked sports-bar-without-the-sports night-club. Pure, without frills—just the way it should be. This is the place to come and genuflect to the guitar. Manny's serves up a mix of journeyman blues acts, local favorites and, every now and then, a grizzled relic from the "Blues Brothers," like Matt "Guitar" Murphy. The

club isn't much bigger than a railroad flat but the weekend warriors crowd is chipper and loud and everyone seems ready to get down and dirty and forget their troubles as quickly as possible.

The high-volume chatter (and the programs issuing from the club's two television sets) bounces off the brick-and-wood walls at maximum velocity. Manny's is filled with black-and-white photographs, Jägermeister posters, and there's a neon sign over the stage that says "BLUES," just in case you forget what the musical theme is.

Nearby: Velvet Room (cocktail lounge with cigar bar) at 209 E. 76th St. bet. Second & Third Aves., 674-7264.

MATCH

Address: 160 Mercer St.
bet. Prince and Houston Sts.
Phone: 343-0020
Hours: Daily, 11:30 A.M. to 4 A.M.
Admission: Free

It might be a little disingenuous to recommend a place that's virtually intolerable six nights a week, but on Sunday, this hip, honey-wood-and-exposed-brick supper club is truly the coolest place in town.

Ignore the chilly hand-blown glass sconces and the shredded aluminum wall fixtures and listen to the voice of Laurel Watson, a spry eighty-seven-year-old chanteuse, as she leads the Shorty Jackson Legacy Band through a set of swinging standards.

The band performs on an elevated metal stage

that resembles a loading dock, and as soon as Laurel steps up to the mike in her red sequined gown, her serene growl and beatific smile hypnotize the chattering crowd and cat-suited waitresses alike.

Match itself is quite sophisticated: the menu is vaguely Asian-multiculti with duck burritos and crab wontons of particular interest. Downstairs there's a slightly less posh lounge where you can recline on leather love seats and drink or have an espresso.

Nearby: Lucky Strike (great late-night french fries) at 59 Grand St. bet. W. Broadway & Wooster St., 941-0479.

THE MERC BAR

Address: 151 Mercer St.
bet. Prince and Houston Sts.
Phone: 966-2727
Hours: Monday and Tuesday, 5 P.M. to 2 A.M.;
Wednesday and Thursday, 5 P.M. to 3 A.M.;
Friday and Saturday, 5 P.M. to 4 A.M.;
Sunday, 6 P.M. to 2 A.M.
Admission: Free

There is a tender moment in a bar's existence when its cachet fades and the bar reluctantly enters the golden years of its career. The Merc Bar is such a place.

Hipness personified a mere year and a half ago, the Merc Bar has become a kinder and gentler, more customer-friendly sort of watering hole. The vampiric Europeans have moved on to more rarefied environs and the ownership seems to have accepted the slightly less-beautiful-but-equally-moneyed mix of Wall Street yups, arty locals, and the dreaded B&T crowd.

The club always had the potential to be comfortable with its homey rafters, woody Twin Peaks-esque ski-lodge decor—note the kayak hanging from the ceiling—but now it's a place where you can find a plush love seat, take off your parka, put your feet up, and fritter away the evening.

Whoever programs the music here has excellent taste and an admirable respect for the lost art of conversation. A quick look around the club confirms it: a genuine sense of calm informs the Merc Bar.

Nearby: Pravda (Russian cocktail lounge) at 281 Lafayette bet. Prince & Houston Sts., 226-4696; Bar 89 (best bathrooms in New York) at 89 Mercer St. bet. Broome & Spring Sts., 274-0989.

MERCURY LOUNGE

Address: 217 E. Houston St.
bet. Ludlow St. and Ave. A
Phone: 260-4700
Hours: Daily, 6 P.M. to 4 A.M.
Showtime: Varies.
Admission: Varies with show.

Thanks to the example set by places like the Mercury Lounge, New York is now experiencing something of a nocturnal renaissance.

In the words of the lounge's owner, "we wanted to create a place where bands felt their music was shown to best advantage and where the audience would also enjoy that same great quality." It's that investment in quality that's paid off in a big way: the club is pleasantly packed every night and has become one of the best places to catch a show.

The sound at the Mercury Lounge is serious business—the club has one of the best P.A. systems in the city. At a private party for Pearl Jam, a member of U2 was heard to call it, "f—-in' brilliant."   And it is.

The Mercury is not large, only two rooms divided by a portal of steel and red velvet. Up front there's a long narrow bar with a generous martini happy hour. In the back, you'll find an exposed brick room where bands of national and local pedigree perform on a spacious, unobstructed stage. If you're out to hear some serious music, this is the place.

Nearby: Max Fish (classic-grunge bar) at 178 Ludlow St. bet. Houston & Stanton, 529-3959; Ludlow Street Café (warm, friendly dive with live bands) at 165 Ludlow St., 353-0536.

THE METROPOLITAN MUSEUM OF ART

Address: Fifth Ave., at 82nd St.
Phone: 535-7710
Hours: Friday and Saturday,
9:30 A.M. to 8:45 P.M.
Suggested Admission: $8, general;
$4, students and seniors.

The extended weekend hours at the Met are probably one of New York's truly best-kept secrets.

✳

Open until 8:45 on Friday and Saturday evenings, the museum usually clears out around seven, and the place becomes, more or less, your own private collection. Wise nocturnal art lovers should arrive just as the daytrippers clear out. Pay the nominal suggested admission (adjusted for a limited visit), pick just one section of the museum (only a fool ventures into the Met without a game plan; you can go back every weekend), and spend

a luxurious hour reading the placards and gazing at the beauty.

After you've had your high-fiber dosage of culture you can repair to one of the Met's several supremely benevolent bar areas for a glass of wine. There's even enough privacy for a little uncultured necking.

After a glass or two, you'll have time for a quick spin through the Temple of Dendur, and still be able to arrive fashionably late to a downtown—where else—dinner party.

Nearby: The Guggenheim Museum (similar weekend hours apply for live jazz) at 1071 Fifth Ave. bet. 88th & 89th Sts., 423-3500.

THE MONKEY BAR

IN THE ELYSÉE HOTEL

Address: 60 E. 54th St.
bet. Madison and Park Aves.
Phone: 838-2600
Hours: Dinner—Monday through Friday, 6 P.M. to
11 P.M.; Friday and Saturday, 6 P.M.
to 11:30 P.M.; Sunday, 5:30 P.M. to 10 P.M.
Bar—Every night until Midnight.
Admission: Free; Jacket required.

Despite a recent photo spread in *The New York Times Magazine* suggesting it's the place for those with "an appetite for mischief," The Monkey Bar has much to recommend it.

First there's the historical angle: in the 30s and 40s, The Monkey Bar entertained all manner of bacchanalian debauches, lewd celebrity trysting, and serious alcoholic adventures. Tennessee Williams met his notorious

end at the hotel and Tallulah Bankhead is rumored to have held a party here wearing nothing but a fur coat.

In the tepid 90s, things are a shade more subdued, but the beautiful people have returned, and they've certainly granted the club a generous dispensation. It's a place to see and be seen in, although occasionally one wonders why. Perhaps it's the undeniable sense that one is part of something important, no matter how fleeting and ersatz. Design flourishes include the obligatory monkey murals, a chichi bar up front, a grand piano, and bar stools shaped like pimientos.

Nearby: Peninsula Hotel (ultra swanky bar) at 700 Fifth Ave., at 55th St., 247-2200.

THE OAK ROOM

AT THE ALGONQUIN HOTEL

Address: 59 W. 44th St.
bet. Fifth and Sixth Aves.
Phone: 840-6800
Hours: Vary, see Showtimes.
Showtimes: Tuesday to Thursday, 9 P.M.;
Friday and Saturday, 9 P.M. and 11:30 P.M.
Closed Sunday and Monday.
Admission: $30-$35 depending on performer;
$15 minimum.
Prices do not include dinner.

The former home of *The New Yorker's* legendary "Round Table" crowd, the Oak Room may have lost its mythic place in American letters—the literary heavyweights can now be found across the street at the Royalton—but it still remains a civilized oasis and a pleasantly frou-frou place to go for drinks, dinner, and a show. The hotel's swank lobby is a quiet place for meditative decompression, and cocktails are available.

The Oak Room, just past the lobby toward the back, is paneled in, as you might have guessed, oak, and the woody atmosphere makes the place feel something like the world's most luxe breakfast nook.

The performers here tend to be hoary veterans from the cabaret or cabaret-jazz world and the prime rib is almost always accompanied by an appetizer of Cole Porter or George Gershwin.

If you're in the mood for a little Dorothy Parker-esque insouciance, try engaging the octogenarian wait staff: they're salty, generous with the liquor, and a barrel of laughs.

Nearby: Coco Pazzo Teatro (chic Northern Italian) west of the Paramount Hotel at 235 W. 46th St. bet. Broadway & Eighth Ave., 827-4222.

PARAMOUNT HOTEL

Address: 235 W. 46th St.
bet. Broadway and Eighth Aves.
Phone: 764-5500
Mezzanine Hours: Sunday through Thursday,
7 A.M. to 1 A.M.;
Friday and Saturday, 7 A.M. to 2 A.M.
Admission: Free

If your dream in life is to beam up into the futuristic world of "Blade Runner," you should visit the Paramount Hotel. The idea of hanging out in a lobby certainly isn't very compelling to most people, but then, the Paramount isn't exactly Motel 6.

In fact the lobby, created by France's design darling, Philippe Starck, is the Paramount's pièce de résistance: check out the curvaceous armchairs with vintage faux-telephones and the dazzling staircase that sweeps across the split-level space. The hotel seems willing to let

you sit, and even nap, undisturbed for hours. If you're hungry, the Paramount has a Dean & Deluca espresso shoppe; if you need a drink, there's a noisy bar, called the Whiskey, packed with Eurotrash; and overlooking the lobby, a comfortably chic restaurant on the mezzanine.

The real pleasure here is to take a private table for two along the lobby's sleek promenade and sit back, look cool, and watch the comings and goings. Starck's high-tech design extends to the bathrooms, which are a marvel of intimidating austerity. But be forewarned, the gender designation is obscurely marked on the floor, and there is a tendency—after a martini or three—to find yourself in the wrong lavatory.

Nearby: Royalton Hotel (Condé Nast hangout) at 44 W. 44th St. bet. Fifth & Sixth Aves., 869-4400.

RAINBOW & STARS
THE RAINBOW ROOM

Address: 30 Rockefeller Plaza
bet. 48th and 49th Sts.
Phone: 632-5100/632-5000
Hours: Rainbow & Stars—Tuesday through
Saturday, 5:30 P.M. to 1 A.M.; Rainbow Room—
Tuesday through Friday, 5:30 P.M. to 1 A.M.;
Saturday, 5:30 P.M. to 2 A.M.
Admission: Rainbow & Stars—$40 plus dinner
(music charge varies); Rainbow Room—$20 music
charge; a la carte menu.

There just isn't anything like it. Sixty-five breath-taking floors above Manhattan, The Rainbow Room and Rainbow & Stars are the musical equivalent of the Empire State Building. Performers at the latter are almost exclusively women of the cabaret and cocktail-jazz persuasion and they're accompanied by a tasteful combo. Most performers have a hard time competing with the panoramic view, so they wisely surrender and work it into the act. The decor here is faux-deco, a vestige of the club's 1940s incarnation. There are cigarette

girls, foil-and-bangle table dressings, and eagle-shaped parapets that line the balustrade.

Down the hall from Rainbow & Stars, and a few decades further back in time, lies the splendor and spectacle of The Rainbow Room, the apex of New York nightlife. The revolving dance floor has been in place since 1934, but watch your step: after a martini it can be hazardous. Set in the center of a kaleidoscopic mirror-and-crystal chandelier ballroom, the dance floor is reached via a curving staircase. There you'll find The Rainbow Room Orchestra—a swinging big band possessed by the spirits of Glenn Miller and Tommy Dorsey. The forties-style microphones and between-song patter are so convincing you'll think Our Boys will be back any day now. Couples find themselves dancing cheek to cheek all night.

ROSELAND

Address: 236 W. 52nd St.
bet. 8th Ave. and Broadway
Phone: 247-0200 (Ballroom)
249-8870 (Concert Hotline)
Hours: Thursday and Sunday,
2:30 P.M. to 11 P.M. for dancing.
Admission: Thursday, $8; Sunday,
$11 for dancing; concert prices vary.

Better known as the Roseland Ballroom, this cavernous bombshelter of a space is perhaps the last of New York's great postwar dance halls. An Atomic Age anachronism, it even smells like the fifties—inside, you expect to see a troupe of Marines dancing gallantly with their gals as they nobly prepare to go off to war. Somewhere in the back there's a bar area that's redolent of ancient bowling alley wax, and even the carpeting predates the Truman administration.

On nights when Roseland isn't open for inno-

cent dancing, it becomes a throbbing rock arena. This is probably because the huge untrammeled space in front of the stage has proved to be the best place in New York for an injury-free mosh pit; bands that demand this sort of devotional fervor are the ones who play here. Sometimes the energy is defused by the sheer vastness of the place; other times, particularly when a band like Tool drops by, the crowd hardens into a solid mass of youthful energy. When you're safely ensconced in the bleachers with the ghost of wallflowers past, it's an amazing thing to witness.

Nearby: Coyote Kate's (Southwest style bar with live bands and an eclectic crowd) at 307 W. 47th St. bet. Eighth and Ninth Aves., 956-1091.

THE ROXY

Address: 515 W. 18th St.
bet. 10th and 11th Aves.
Phone: 645-5156
Hours: Varies each night (call to check).
Closed Sunday.
Admission: $12 to $20, depending on night.

A walk up the Roxy's long black stairway is like a trip down Memory Lane: the Roxy is actually the last surviving mega-club from the heady days of the late seventies when Warhol and Bianca Jagger ruled New York. The Roxy's longevity probably has a lot to do with the fact that it's also a roller disco, a novelty less prevalent than one might suspect in a city of this size.

Both in-line and old-fashioned skating go down on Tuesday and Wednesday (Tuesday is gay, Wednesday is straight. House music doesn't sound particularly good in this black-on-

black hanger-sized space, but they play it so loud your skates start spinning from the vibrations. The crowd is exquisitely diverse—on a good night you'll find hot-shot club kids skating alongside old-timers from the golden age of Polka.

When dizziness sets in there are several lounges in which to decompress. On Saturday the club locks up their skates and forces the mixed crowd to demonstrate some pure pelvic innovation.

Nearby: La Luncheonette (comfy, ultra Westside bistro) at Tenth Ave. at 18th St., 675-0342; Alley's End (vast grotto serves new American food) at 311 W. 17th St. bet. Eighth & Ninth Aves., 627-8899.

SIDEWALK

Address: 94 Avenue A at 6th St.
Phone: 473-7373
Hours: Open 24 hours.
Admission: For musical performances,
there's a one-drink minimum.

More fashionable destinations may come and go, but there are few clubs in New York as comfy as this sprawling East Village bar, grill, pool hall, and performance space.

Don't expect much in the way of glamour here. There's a inexplicable bird-of-prey motif at the small bar (happy hour is from 2 P.M.-8 P.M. daily), turquoise Christmas lights, irresistible bowls filled with roasted peanuts (a sign says please keep the shells on the floor. Where else would you put them?), two TVs set to Nickelodeon, exposed brick, little red votives, good food (cheap burgers, salads, sandwiches),

competent, no-nonsense waitresses, preppies, punks, Rastas, and a vintage valet parking sign. There's never a cover charge at Sidewalk, and in a backroom performance area called "The Fort," on a small stage with decorative flugel-horns glued to the wall (and eggshell-box soundproofing the ceiling), you can hear some of the best acoustic music in town, seven night a week.

Nearby: O.G.'s (Pan-Asian grill) at 507 E. 6th St. bet. Aves. A & B, 477-4649; Nation (nightly deejays) at 50 Ave. A bet. 3rd & 4th Sts., 473-6239.

S.O.B.'S

(S O U N D S   O F   B R A Z I L)

**Address: 204 Varick St.,
corner of West Houston St.
Phone: 243-4940
Hours: vary; call to check.
Admission: $12 to $20 (Prices vary; call to check).**

Like a night-club as conceived by Carmen Miranda, S.O.B.'s might be best described as neo-tropical.

The walls have been painted in a lurid fruit motif; there are stuffed exotic birds, bamboo scaffolding, and a mock thatched roof ceiling—all of which makes for a festive and slightly daunting experience. African, Afro-Caribbean, reggae and world-beat fill the docket. The Brazilian influence extends to the menu, which features delicious Portuguese specialties. A dance floor in front of the stage is encircled by a cabaña-like bar.

On Mondays, for a nominal admission charge, you can get salsa dancing lessons and then stay for the night's concert—one of the best bargains in the city. On Tuesday evenings, the club enjoys a particularly grueling workout when Frankie Jackson's Soul Kitchen arrives. Currently based here, Soul Kitchen is a night of classic disco and funk from the seventies with all the necessary accoutrements: lava lamps, a few turntables and black-light posters with phrases like "Right On." Don't bother showing up before midnight; things get started late. Expect to hear the "Shaft" theme and other chestnuts.

The chicken wings are gratis and the Colt .45 reasonably priced.

Nearby: Film Forum (art and revival cinema), at 209 W. Houston bet. Sixth Ave. & Varick St., 927-8110; Buddha Bar (Tribeca hipster lounge) at 150 Varick St. bet. Vandam & Spring Sts., 255-4433.

SWEET BASIL

**Address: 88 Seventh Ave. South,
bet. Bleecker and Grove Sts.
Phone: 242-1785
Hours: Monday through Thursday, 5 P.M. to
12:30 P.M.; Friday and Saturday, Noon to
1:30A.M., Sunday, Noon to 12:30 A.M.
Showtimes: Sunday through Thursday,
9 P.M. and 11 P.M.; Friday and Saturday,
9 P.M., 11 P.M., 12:30 A.M.;
Admission: $17.50 cover
plus $10 minimum food and drink.**

If you're one of those people who thinks the measure of a jazz club's greatness lies in the number of photographs on its wall, then you'll love Sweet Basil. Virtually every inch of wall space in this old wood-and-brick workhorse is covered with the smiling faces of former clients from the late, great Dizzy Gillespie to Wynton Marsalis.

Sweet Basil may have less seniority than the Village Vanguard and lack the gloss and glitter

of fledgling jazz clubs like Iridium and Metropolis, but it remains an internationally renowned venue and books jazz greats from all over the world. Everyone who's Anyone has played Sweet Basil at one time or another and the list of "Live at Sweet Basil" records is daunting.

The club itself is small, close, and extremely informal with a bar toward the front and a no-frills kitchen in the back (Tip: Come for the jazz, have dinner elsewhere.)

A dozen tables surround the tiny stage—there's not a bad seat in the house—and if you don't want a trumpet blaring in your ear, there are a few more tables in a comfortable glass-enclosed "patio."

Nearby: The Bitter End (good local bands) at 149 Bleecker St. at Thompson St., 673-7030.

TENTH STREET LOUNGE

Address: 212 E. 10th bet. First and Second Aves.
Phone: 473-5252
Hours: Tuesday through Saturday, 5 P.M. to 3 A.M.;
Sunday, 4:30 P.M. to 2 A.M.
Admission: Thursday through Saturday, $10 cover
(varies; call to check).

Never ever come here on weekends: it's probably a truism applicable to all the clubs in the book, but at the Tenth Street Lounge it will save you ten bucks—because that's the nasty opportunistic cover they charge to keep the crowds at bay. The rest of the week though, when the hordes are safely tucked in bed, this cavernous, cathedral-ceilinged space, done in severe white cinder block and exposed brick and lit with the glow of millions of votive candles, is still one of the coolest places in town.

In the summer the bar throws open its huge polished metal doors, a cool breeze blows in

through the front room, and an alluring smoky orange haze floods out into the street. In the winter, the bar can be a little hard to spot. Look for the gleaming doors that look so out of place in the East Village, and the hip-looking crowd milling outside.

Try stopping by, say, around two a.m. on a torrid weeknight—it's a highly evolved form of decompression.

Nearby: Shabu-Tatsu (do-it-yourself Japanese BBQ) at 216 E. 10th St. bet. First & Second Aves., 477-2972; Flamingo East (dining with late-night dj) at 219 Second Ave. bet. 13th & 14th Sts., 533-2860; Orson's (small cocktail bar) at 175 Second Ave. bet. 11th & 12th Sts., 475-1530.

TRAMPS

Address: 51 W. 21st St. bet. Fifth and Sixth Aves.
Phone: 727-7788
Hours: Thursday through Saturday,
7:30 P.M. to 4 A.M.
Admission: $5 to $20 (varies; call to check).

Fancier, trendier clubs may come and go, but Tramps endures. It probably has a lot to do with the fortitude and professionalism of Tramps' owner, an Irish émigré with a distaste for pretension and a passion for the Blues, Zydeco, and many other American music forms from west of the Mississippi.

The aesthetic at this spacious high school gym of a club is minimal. All you'll find in the way of affectation are a few posters, a colorless drum set, and an accordion in the window. The sightlines at Tramps are slightly compromised by a few ill-considered columns, and the sound is occasionally dull and woolly, but the club

perpetually lures an unpredictable, top-notch group of headliners. Hard working rockers like the Subdudes will play one night, followed by alternative darlings like Sebadoh, who might then easily be followed by a country-and-Western act like the Mavericks. Anything goes.

If you're feeling under musical attack at Tramps, you can always take shelter by walking up to the huge rear bar that wraps around the far end of the club—or cut across the street to Chelsea Billiards for a quick game of Eight Ball.

A new annex called Tramps Café is a small contiguous space with an emphasis on South-western cooking and more modest singer-song-writer and blues acts.

Nearby: Thiasos (Greek night club) at 59 W. 21st St. bet. Fifth & Sixth Aves., 727-7775.

VILLAGE GATE

Address: 240 W. 52nd St.
bet. Broadway and Eighth Ave.
Phone: 307-5252
Hours: Dinner starting at 6 P.M.;
Showtimes: Tuesday through Saturday, 8:15 P.M.;
Sunday, 7:15 P.M.; Live jazz and dancing from
10 P.M. to 2 A.M.; closed Mondays
Admission: $55 for dinner and show package,
$40 for show; $10 for jazz with a 2 drink
minimum on Saturday,
$5 for jazz Tuesday through Friday.

Like its older, more respectable cousin, the Village Vanguard, the Village Gate was once a bright light on the downtown radar screen. Over the years, the enormous space was home to everything from high-profile jazz gigs to theatrical revues. When the tourist scene of Bleecker Street fell upon hard times, the Gate was one of the area's most conspicuous casualties. This tragic bit of news was recently erased when the club reopened—surprise!—smack in the middle of Times Square.

If the new space leaves a little to be desired by way of charm and history, it gets an "A" for effort in the comfort department: upstairs, there's a quiet, non-working fireplace, wood floors, votive candles, fancy fixtures, and a quiet bar area far from the stage where you can enjoy a relaxing rec room sort of vibe. The walls are exposed brick and they're draped with plush red-velvet curtains. A series of dinner tables (with real tableclothes, something you'd never find in the old Gate) afford a great bird's-eye view from above; you can also sit downstairs. The stage has a garish, Erté meets Art Deco motif, but the rest of the place is peppered with tasteful black-and-white photos of the famous musicians who are destined to return. Welcome back.

Nearby: Le Bar Bat (plenty of action with dining, disco, djs, and live music) at 311 W. 57th St. bet. Eighth & Ninth Aves., 307-7228.

VILLAGE VANGUARD

Address: 178 Seventh Ave. S.
bet. Waverly and 11th Sts.
Phone: 255-4037
Hours: Vary, (call to check).
Showtimes: Varies with performers.
Admission: Varies with performers;
$10 minimum for drinks.

The closest thing we have to a glorified jazz museum, this subterranean landmark is also the eminence grise of New York nightclubs: it's over sixty years old and still going strong.

Set in a dark and musty basement, the Vanguard isn't much in the way of pomp and circumstance—it's smoky, crowded, and dusty—but the fossilized clubhouse atmosphere never seems to bother anyone. Every nook and cranny at the Vanguard has its own hoary anecdote. There's a perpetually broken

light fixture, for instance, that's rumored to be the work of a very angry Charles Mingus, and the club has no intention of fixing it.

The Vanguard is almost exclusively a jazz club, but unusual alumni include the poet and Gap spokesperson Allen Ginsberg, who read selections from "Howl," to a crowd of bongo-mellowed beatniks in the late sixties.

The Vanguard is still firmly ensconced at the top of every international tourist guide: the crowd is like a U.N. meeting, but the mood, thanks to the music, remains one of global fraternity.

Nearby: John's Pizza (best pizza in NYC) at 278 Bleecker St. bet. Sixth & Seventh Aves., 243-1680.

WEBSTER HALL

Address: 125 E. 11th St.
bet. Third and Fourth Aves.
Phone: 353-1600
Hours: Thursday through Saturday,
10 P.M. to 5 A.M.
Admission: $20.

Someday a thoughtful grad student will write a dissertation on the disco as theme park, and Webster Hall will be the model. With the possible exception of the Palladium, Webster Hall is a prototype of awe-inspiring grandiosity in the Trumpian spirit of one-upmanship.

In terms of nocturnal square-footage, the Hall is huge: there are four fully-functioning floors, and as you move up and down the staircase, you discover each level has its own distinct flavor. (One can't help feeling there must be another floor available for V.I.P.s.)

On any given night you can hear everything from acid jazz to Aerosmith to reggae, depending on your longitude and latitude. The place is so immense it's probably not a bad idea to bring your own walkie-talkies—if you and your crew can get them past the bouncers.

The primary area features a hangar-sized dance floor, apocalyptic lighting, and a big stage for live performance—grunge bands play on Thursdays; Wednesday is drag night. If you get peckish from all the walking around, don't worry; there's a coffee shop. If you're having a bad hair day, take heart; there's a wig boutique in the basement.

Nearby: Continental Divide (classic East Village rock venue) at 25 Third Ave. at St. Marks Pl., 529-6924.

WETLANDS

Address: 161 Hudson St. bet. Laight and Hubert Sts.
Phone: 966-4225
Hours: Monday through Wednesday, 5 P.M. to
2 A.M.; Thursday through Saturday, 9 P.M. to
4 A.M.; Sunday, 5 P.M. to 12 A.M.
Admission: Varies (call to check);
Tuesday, no charge.

The only club in the city with a disemboweled Volkswagen bus parked on the dance floor, Wetlands remains the headquarters of the tie-dye and environmentally-aware set.

A laudable, if somewhat ersatz, New Age spirit informs everything this sprawling club does. You'll find leaflets on interesting programs like recycling, PETA, fasting, and the local Greenpeace branch meeting place next week. There's a distribution desk for materials from international fringe organizations and other volunteer programs available from the wide-eyed staff

who make their headquarters inside the VW.

The music at Wetlands tends to focus primarily on jam-happy teenage bands weaned on Grateful Dead records, and they have huge, affluent, and highly educated followings. Sandals and loose-fitting clothing are de rigueur. The club is like a colossal college dorm: there are lots of wood columns to lean against and ephemera from the Summer of Love.

Downstairs a cavernous area is divided into small rooms where the youthful crowd hangs out, and one frequently spies a bit of furtive necking and smells the unmistakable fragrances of a certain holistic remedy.

Nearby: Nobu (posh Japanese restaurant) at 105 Hudson St. at Franklin St., 219-0500.

WORLD YACHT

Address: Pier 81—W. 41st St. at Twelfth Ave.
Phone: 630-8100
Hours: Monday through Sunday dinner sails,
7 P.M. to 10 P.M.
Admission: Sunday through Friday,
$70 per person; Saturday, $84.

Like a floating luxury hotel suite, the World Yacht is perfect for rocky relationships and Gilligan's Island fanatics. This soothing three-hour tour includes a sit-down dinner (the chef's from Burgundy), dancing to live jazz, drinks (for a wee bit extra), and unrivaled panoramic views of the Big Apple.

The World Yacht's fleet includes five three-level Love Boats—each is a riot of maroon carpeting, mirrors, gold-plated fixtures, and fake potted plants. The boats seat seventy to four hundred and sail year-round (on weekends in the winter; seven days a week in the summer).

It's a long, leisurely three hours: no one ever gets rushed from the table. In clement weather you can head up top and let the wind muss your hair as the boat meanders south to the Battery, swings uptown past the Brooklyn Bridge to twenty-third Street, and then crawls back home—with a brief photo opportunity at the base of the Statue of Liberty. Most people seem to charter the World Yacht for special occasions: weddings, Fourth of July, Bar Mitzvahs, anniversaries, etc. Bruce Willis once hosted a wrap party here. But this is a mistake—the World Yacht experience is best enjoyed as a weeknight whim (besides, reservations for the weekends fill up weeks in advance). Ahoy, matey.

Nearby: The Circle Line (cruise and eat hot dogs).

Index

ABOUT THE AUTHOR

Andrew Essex is the nightlife editor at *The New Yorker*. He lives in Manhattan.

D1364315